The Poetry of Alexander Pope

Volume II

Alexander Pope was born on May 21st, 1688 in London into a Catholic family.

His education was affected by the recent Test Acts, upholding the status of the Church of England and banning Catholics from teaching. In effect this meant his formal education was over by the age of 12 and Pope was to now immerse himself in classical literature and languages and to, in effect, educate himself.

From this age too he also suffered from numerous health problems including a type of tuberculosis (Pott's disease) which resulted in a stunted, deformed body. Only to grow to a height of 4' 6", with a severe hunchback and complicated further by respiratory difficulties, high fevers, inflamed eyes and abdominal pain all of which served to further isolate him, initially, from society.

However his talent was evident to all. Best known for his satirical verse, his translations of Homer and the use of the heroic couplet, he is the second-most frequently quoted writer in The Oxford Dictionary of Quotations, after Shakespeare.

With the publication of Pastorals in 1709 followed by An Essay on Criticism (1711) and his most famous work The Rape of the Lock (1712; revised and enlarged in 1714) Pope became not only famous but wealthy.

His translations of the Iliad and the Odyssey further enhanced both reputation and purse. His engagement to produce an opulent new edition of Shakespeare met with a mixed reception. Pope attempted to "regularise" Shakespeare's metre and rewrote some of his verse and cut 1500 lines, that Pope considered to be beneath the Bard's standard, to mere footnotes.

Alexander Pope died on May 30th, 1744 at his villa at Twickenham (where he created his famous grotto and gardens) and was buried in the nave of the nearby Church of England Church of St Mary the Virgin.

Over the years and centuries since his death Pope's work has been in and out of favour but with this distance he is now truly recognised as one of England's greatest poets.

Index of Contents

To Mrs Arabella Fermor
THE RAPE OF THE LOCK
Canto I
Canto II
Canto III
Canto IV
Canto V
PASTORALS
Pastorals – With a Discourse on Pastoral Poetry

Spring, the First Pastoral, or Damon
Summer, the Second Pastoral, or Alexis
Autumn, the Third Pastoral, or Hylas and Ægon
Winter, the Fourth Pastoral, or Daphne
Alexander Pope – A Short Biography
Alexander Pope – A Concise Bibliography

'Nolueram, Belinda, tuos violare capillos;
Sed juvat, hoc precibus me tribuisse tuis.'
MART.

TO MRS ARABELLA FERMOR

Madam, It will be in vain to deny that I have some regard for this piece, since I dedicate it to you. Yet you may bear me witness, it was intended only to divert a few young ladies, who have good sense and good-humour enough to laugh not only at their sex's little unguarded follies, but at their own. But as it was communicated with the air of a secret, it soon found its way into the world. An imperfect copy having been offered to a bookseller, you had the good-nature for my sake to consent to the publication of one more correct: this I was forced to, before I had executed half my design, for the machinery was entirely wanting to complete it.

The machinery, Madam, is a term invented by the critics, to signify that part which the deities, angels, or demons are made to act in a poem: for the ancient poets are in one respect like many modern ladies: let an action be never so trivial in itself, they always make it appear of the utmost importance. These machines I determined to raise on a very new and odd foundation—the Rosicrucian doctrine of spirits.

I know how disagreeable it is to make use of hard words before a lady; but 'tis so much the concern of a poet to have his works understood, and particularly by your sex, that you must give me leave to explain two or three difficult terms.

The Rosicrucians are a people I must bring you acquainted with. The best account I know of them is in a French book called 'Le Comte de Gabalis,' which both in its title and size is so like a novel, that many of the fair sex have read it for one by mistake. According to these gentlemen, the four elements are inhabited by spirits, which they call Sylphs, Gnomes, Nymphs, and Salamanders. The Gnomes, or Demons of Earth, delight in mischief; but the Sylphs, whose habitation is in the air, are the best-conditioned creatures imaginable. For they say, any mortals may enjoy the most intimate familiarities with these gentle spirits, upon a condition very easy to all true adepts—an inviolate preservation of chastity.

As to the following cantos, all the passages of them are as fabulous as the vision at the beginning, or the transformation at the end; (except the loss of your hair, which I always mention with reverence). The human persons are as fictitious as the airy ones; and the character of Belinda, as it is now managed, resembles you in nothing but in beauty. If this poem had as many graces as there are in your person, or in your mind, yet I could never hope it should pass through the world half so uncensured as you have done. But let its fortune be what it will, mine is happy enough to have given me this occasion of assuring you that I am, with the truest esteem, Madam, your most obedient, humble servant,

A. POPE.

CANTO I

What dire offence from amorous causes springs,
What mighty contests rise from trivial things,
I sing—This verse to Caryll, Muse! is due:
This, even Belinda may vouchsafe to view:
Slight is the subject, but not so the praise,
If she inspire, and he approve my lays.

Say what strange motive, Goddess! could compel
A well-bred lord t'assault a gentle belle?
Oh, say what stranger cause, yet unexplored,
Could make a gentle belle reject a lord?
In tasks so bold, can little men engage,
And in soft bosoms dwells such mighty rage?

Sol through white curtains shot a timorous ray,
And oped those eyes that must eclipse the day:
Now lap-dogs give themselves the rousing shake,
And sleepless lovers, just at twelve, awake:
Thrice rung the bell, the slipper knock'd the ground,
And the press'd watch return'd a silver sound.
Belinda still her downy pillow press'd,
Her guardian Sylph prolong'd the balmy rest:
'Twas he had summon'd to her silent bed
The morning-dream that hover'd o'er her head,
A youth more glittering than a birth-night beau,
(That even in slumber caused her cheek to glow),
Seem'd to her ear his willing lips to lay,
And thus in whispers said, or seem'd to say:

'Fairest of mortals, thou distinguish'd care
Of thousand bright inhabitants of air!
If e'er one vision touch thy infant thought,
Of all the nurse and all the priest have taught;
Of airy elves by moonlight shadows seen,
The silver token, and the circled green,
Or virgins visited by angel-powers,
With golden crowns and wreaths of heavenly flowers;
Hear and believe! thy own importance know,
Nor bound thy narrow views to things below.
Some secret truths, from learned pride conceal'd,

To maids alone and children are reveal'd:
What though no credit doubting wits may give?
The fair and innocent shall still believe.
Know then, unnumber'd spirits round thee fly,
The light militia of the lower sky:
These, though unseen, are ever on the wing,
Hang o'er the box, and hover round the ring.
Think what an equipage thou hast in air,
And view with scorn two pages and a chair.
As now your own, our beings were of old,
And once enclosed in woman's beauteous mould;
Thence, by a soft transition, we repair
From earthly vehicles to these of air.
Think not, when woman's transient breath is fled,
That all her vanities at once are dead;
Succeeding vanities she still regards,
And though she plays no more, o'erlooks the cards.
Her joy in gilded chariots, when alive,
And love of ombre, after death survive.
For when the fair in all their pride expire,
To their first elements their souls retire:
The sprites of fiery termagants in flame
Mount up, and take a Salamander's name.
Soft yielding minds to water glide away,
And sip, with Nymphs, their elemental tea.
The graver prude sinks downward to a Gnome,
In search of mischief still on earth to roam.
The light coquettes in Sylphs aloft repair,
And sport and flutter in the fields of air.

'Know further yet; whoever fair and chaste
Rejects mankind, is by some Sylph embraced:
For spirits, freed from mortal laws, with ease
Assume what sexes and what shapes they please.
What guards the purity of melting maids,
In courtly balls, and midnight masquerades,
Safe from the treacherous friend, the daring spark,
The glance by day, the whisper in the dark,
When kind occasion prompts their warm desires,
When music softens, and when dancing fires?
'Tis but their Sylph, the wise celestials know,
Though honour is the word with men below.

'Some nymphs there are, too conscious of their face,
For life predestined to the Gnomes' embrace.
These swell their prospects, and exalt their pride,
When offers are disdain'd, and love denied;
Then gay ideas crowd the vacant brain,

While peers, and dukes, and all their sweeping train,
And garters, stars, and coronets appear,
And in soft sounds, 'Your Grace' salutes their ear.
'Tis these that early taint the female soul,
Instruct the eyes of young coquettes to roll,
Teach infant cheeks a bidden blush to know,
And little hearts to flutter at a beau.

'Oft, when the world imagine women stray,
The Sylphs through mystic mazes guide their way,
Through all the giddy circle they pursue,
And old impertinence expel by new.
What tender maid but must a victim fall
To one man's treat, but for another's ball?
When Florio speaks, what virgin could withstand,
If gentle Damon did not squeeze her hand?
With varying vanities, from every part,
They shift the moving toyshop of their heart,
Where wigs with wigs, with sword-knots sword-knots strive,
Beaux banish beaux, and coaches coaches drive.
This erring mortals levity may call,
Oh, blind to truth! the Sylphs contrive it all.

'Of these am I, who thy protection claim,
A watchful sprite, and Ariel is my name.
Late, as I ranged the crystal wilds of air,
In the clear mirror of thy ruling star
I saw, alas! some dread event impend,
Ere to the main this morning sun descend,
But heaven reveals not what, or how, or where:
Warn'd by the Sylph, oh, pious maid, beware!
This to disclose is all thy guardian can:
Beware of all, but most beware of man!'

He said; when Shock, who thought she slept too long,
Leap'd up, and waked his mistress with his tongue.
'Twas then, Belinda, if report say true,
Thy eyes first open'd on a billet-doux;
Wounds, charms, and ardours, were no sooner read,
But all the vision vanish'd from thy head.

And now, unveil'd, the toilet stands display'd,
Each silver vase in mystic order laid.
First, robed in white, the nymph intent adores,
With head uncover'd, the cosmetic powers.
A heavenly image in the glass appears,
To that she bends, to that her eyes she rears;
The inferior priestess, at her altar's side,

Trembling, begins the sacred rites of pride.
Unnumber'd treasures ope at once, and here
The various offerings of the world appear;
From each she nicely culls with curious toil,
And decks the goddess with the glittering spoil.
This casket India's glowing gems unlocks,
And all Arabia breathes from yonder box.
The tortoise here, and elephant unite,
Transform'd to combs, the speckled and the white.
Here files of pins extend their shining rows,
Puffs, powders, patches, Bibles, billet-doux.
Now awful beauty puts on all its arms;
The fair each moment rises in her charms,
Repairs her smiles, awakens every grace,
And calls forth all the wonders of her face;
Sees by degrees a purer blush arise,
And keener lightnings quicken in her eyes.
The busy Sylphs surround their darling care,
These set the head, and those divide the hair,
Some fold the sleeve, whilst others plait the gown:
And Betty's praised for labours not her own.

CANTO II

Not with more glories, in the ethereal plain,
The sun first rises o'er the purpled main,
Than, issuing forth, the rival of his beams
Launched on the bosom of the silver Thames.
Fair nymphs and well-dress'd youths around her shone,
But every eye was fix'd on her alone.
On her white breast a sparkling cross she wore,
Which Jews might kiss, and infidels adore.
Her lively looks a sprightly mind disclose,
Quick as her eyes, and as unfix'd as those:
Favours to none, to all she smiles extends;
Oft she rejects, but never once offends.
Bright as the sun, her eyes the gazers strike,
And, like the sun, they shine on all alike.
Yet graceful ease, and sweetness void of pride
Might hide her faults, if belles had faults to hide:
If to her share some female errors fall,
Look on her face, and you'll forget 'em all.

This nymph, to the destruction of mankind,
Nourish'd two locks, which graceful hung behind
In equal curls, and well conspired to deck

With shining ringlets the smooth ivory neck.
Love in these labyrinths his slaves detains,
And mighty hearts are held in slender chains.
With hairy springes we the birds betray,
Slight lines of hair surprise the finny prey,
Fair tresses man's imperial race ensnare,
And beauty draws us with a single hair.

The adventurous Baron the bright locks admired;
He saw, he wished, and to the prize aspired.
Resolved to win, he meditates the way,
By force to ravish, or by fraud betray;
For when success a lover's toil attends,
Few ask if fraud or force attain'd his ends.

For this, ere Phoebus rose, he had implored
Propitious Heaven, and every power adored,
But chiefly Love—to Love an altar built,
Of twelve vast French romances, neatly gilt.
There lay three garters, half a pair of gloves;
And all the trophies of his former loves;
With tender billet-doux he lights the pyre,
And breathes three amorous sighs to raise the fire.
Then prostrate falls, and begs with ardent eyes
Soon to obtain, and long possess the prize:
The powers gave ear, and granted half his prayer,
The rest, the winds dispersed in empty air.

But now secure the painted vessel glides,
The sunbeams trembling on the floating tides:
While melting music steals upon the sky,
And soften'd sounds along the waters die;
Smooth flow the waves, the zephyrs gently play,
Belinda smiled, and all the world was gay.
All but the Sylph—with careful thoughts oppress'd,
The impending woe sat heavy on his breast.
He summons straight his denizens of air;
The lucid squadrons round the sails repair;
Soft o'er the shrouds aërial whispers breathe,
That seem'd but zephyrs to the train beneath.
Some to the sun their insect-wings unfold,
Waft on the breeze, or sink in clouds of gold;
Transparent forms, too fine for mortal sight,
Their fluid bodies half dissolved in light.
Loose to the wind their airy garments flew,
Thin glittering textures of the filmy dew,
Dipp'd in the richest tincture of the skies,
Where light disports in ever-mingling dyes;

While every beam new transient colours flings,
Colours that change whene'er they wave their wings.
Amid the circle, on the gilded mast,
Superior by the head, was Ariel placed;
His purple pinions opening to the sun,
He raised his azure wand, and thus begun:

'Ye Sylphs and Sylphids, to your chief give ear,
Fays, fairies, genii, elves, and demons hear!
Ye know the spheres, and various tasks assign'd
By laws eternal to the aërial kind.
Some in the fields of purest ether play,
And bask and whiten in the blaze of day:
Some guide the course of wandering orbs on high,
Or roll the planets through the boundless sky:
Some, less refined, beneath the moon's pale light
Pursue the stars that shoot athwart the night,
Or suck the mists in grosser air below,
Or dip their pinions in the painted bow,
Or brew fierce tempests on the wintry main,
Or o'er the glebe distil the kindly rain.
Others on earth o'er human race preside,
Watch all their ways, and all their actions guide:
Of these the chief the care of nations own,
And guard with arms divine the British throne.

'Our humbler province is to tend the fair,
Not a less pleasing, though less glorious care;
To save the powder from too rude a gale,
Nor let the imprison'd essences exhale;
To draw fresh colours from the vernal flowers;
To steal from rainbows, ere they drop in showers,
A brighter wash; to curl their waving hairs,
Assist their blushes, and inspire their airs;
Nay, oft, in dreams, invention we bestow,
To change a flounce, or add a furbelow.

'This day, black omens threat the brightest fair
That e'er deserved a watchful spirit's care;
Some dire disaster, or by force, or flight;
But what, or where, the Fates have wrapt in night.
Whether the nymph shall break Diana's law,
Or some frail China jar receive a flaw;
Or stain her honour, or her new brocade;
Forget her prayers, or miss a masquerade;
Or lose her heart, or necklace, at a ball;
Or whether Heaven has doom'd that Shock must fall,
Haste then, ye spirits! to your charge repair:

The fluttering fan be Zephyretta's care;
The drops to thee, Brillante, we consign;
And, Momentilla, let the watch be thine;
Do thou, Crispissa, tend her favourite lock;
Ariel himself shall be the guard of Shock.

'To fifty chosen Sylphs, of special note,
We trust the important charge, the petticoat:
Oft have we known that sevenfold fence to fail,
Though stiff with hoops, and arm'd with ribs of whale;
Form a strong line about the silver bound,
And guard the wide circumference around.

'Whatever spirit, careless of his charge,
His post neglects, or leaves the fair at large,
Shall feel sharp vengeance soon o'ertake his sins,
Be stopp'd in vials, or transfix'd with pins;
Or plunged in lakes of bitter washes lie,
Or wedged whole ages in a bodkin's eye:
Gums and pomatums shall his flight restrain,
While, clogg'd, he beats his silken wings in vain;
Or alum styptics with contracting power
Shrink his thin essence like a rivell'd flower:
Or, as Ixion fix'd, the wretch shall feel
The giddy motion of the whirling mill,
In fumes of burning chocolate shall glow,
And tremble at the sea that froths below!'

He spoke; the spirits from the sails descend;
Some, orb in orb, around the nymph extend;
Some thread the mazy ringlets of her hair;
Some hang upon the pendants of her ear;
With beating hearts the dire event they wait,
Anxious, and trembling for the birth of Fate.

CANTO III

Close by those meads, for ever crown'd with flowers,
Where Thames with pride surveys his rising towers,
There stands a structure of majestic frame,
Which from the neighb'ring Hampton takes its name.
Here Britain's statesmen oft the fall foredoom
Of foreign tyrants, and of nymphs at home;
Here thou, great Anna! whom three realms obey,
Dost sometimes counsel take—and sometimes tea.

Hither the heroes and the nymphs resort,
To taste awhile the pleasures of a court;
In various talk the instructive hours they pass'd,
Who gave the ball, or paid the visit last;
One speaks the glory of the British Queen,
And one describes a charming Indian screen;
A third interprets motions, looks, and eyes;
At every word a reputation dies.
Snuff, or the fan, supply each pause of chat,
With singing, laughing, ogling, and all that.

Meanwhile, declining from the noon of day,
The sun obliquely shoots his burning ray;
The hungry judges soon the sentence sign,
And wretches hang that jurymen may dine;
The merchant from the Exchange returns in peace,
And the long labours of the toilet cease.
Belinda now, whom thirst of fame invites,
Burns to encounter two adventurous knights,
At ombre singly to decide their doom,
And swells her breast with conquests yet to come.
Straight the three bands prepare in arras to join,
Each band the number of the sacred Nine.
Soon as she spreads her hand, the aërial guard
Descend, and sit on each important card:
First Ariel perch'd upon a Matadore,
Then each, according to the rank they bore;
For Sylphs, yet mindful of their ancient race,
Are, as when women, wondrous fond of place.

Behold, four Kings in majesty revered,
With hoary whiskers and a forky beard;
And four fair Queens, whose hands sustain a flower,
Th' expressive emblem of their softer power;
Four Knaves in garbs succinct, a trusty band,
Caps on their heads, and halberts in their hand;
And particolour'd troops, a shining train,
Draw forth to combat on the velvet plain.

The skilful nymph reviews her force with care:
'Let Spades be Trumps!' she said, and Trumps they were.

Now move to war her sable Matadores,
In show like leaders of the swarthy Moors.
Spadillio first, unconquerable lord!
Led off two captive Trumps, and swept the board.
As many more Manillio forced to yield,
And march'd a victor from the verdant field.

Him Basto follow'd, but his fate more hard
Gain'd but one Trump and one plebeian card.
With his broad sabre next, a chief in years,
The hoary Majesty of Spades appears,
Puts forth one manly leg, to sight reveal'd,
The rest, his many-colour'd robe conceal'd.
The rebel Knave, who dares his prince engage,
Proves the just victim of his royal rage.
Even mighty Pam, that Kings and Queens o'erthrew
And mow'd down armies in the fights of Loo,
Sad chance of war! now destitute of aid,
Falls undistinguish'd by the victor Spade!

Thus far both armies to Belinda yield;
Now to the Baron fate inclines the field.
His warlike Amazon her host invades,
The imperial consort of the crown of Spades.
The Club's black tyrant first her victim died,
Spite of his haughty mien, and barbarous pride:
What boots the regal circle on his head,
His giant limbs in state unwieldy spread;
That long behind he trails his pompous robe,
And, of all monarchs, only grasps the globe?

The Baron now his Diamonds pours apace;
The embroider'd King who shows but half his face,
And his refulgent Queen, with powers combined,
Of broken troops an easy conquest find.
Clubs, Diamonds, Hearts, in wild disorder seen,
With throngs promiscuous strew the level green.
Thus when dispersed a routed army runs,
Of Asia's troops, and Afric's sable sons,
With like confusion different nations fly,
Of various habit and of various dye;
The pierced battalions disunited fall
In heaps on heaps; one fate o'erwhelms them all.

The Knave of Diamonds tries his wily arts,
And wins (oh shameful chance!) the Queen of Hearts.
At this, the blood the virgin's cheek forsook,
A livid paleness spreads o'er all her look;
She sees, and trembles at the approaching ill,
Just in the jaws of ruin, and Codille.
And now, (as oft in some distemper'd state)
On one nice trick depends the general fate,
An Ace of Hearts steps forth: the King unseen
Lurk'd in her hand, and mourn'd his captive Queen:
He springs to vengeance with an eager pace,

And falls like thunder on the prostrate Ace.
The nymph, exulting, fills with shouts the sky;
The walls, the woods, and long canals reply.

O thoughtless mortals! ever blind to fate,
Too soon dejected, and too soon elate.
Sudden these honours shall be snatch'd away,
And cursed for ever this victorious day.

For lo! the board with cups and spoons is crown'd,
The berries crackle, and the mill turns round;
On shining altars of Japan they raise
The silver lamp; the fiery spirits blaze:
From silver spouts the grateful liquors glide,
While China's earth receives the smoking tide:
At once they gratify their scent and taste,
And frequent cups prolong the rich repast.
Straight hover round the fair her airy band;
Some, as she sipp'd, the fuming liquor fann'd,
Some o'er her lap their careful plumes display'd,
Trembling, and conscious of the rich brocade.
Coffee (which makes the politician wise,
And see through all things with his half-shut eyes)
Sent up in vapours to the Baron's brain
New stratagems, the radiant lock to gain.
Ah, cease, rash youth! desist ere 'tis too late,
Fear the just gods, and think of Scylla's fate!
Changed to a bird, and sent to flit in air,
She dearly pays for Nisus' injured hair!

But when to mischief mortals bend their will,
How soon they find fit instruments of ill!
Just then, Clarissa drew with tempting grace
A two-edged weapon from her shining case:
So ladies in romance assist their knight,
Present the spear, and arm him for the fight,
He takes the gift with reverence, and extends
The little engine on his fingers' ends:
This just behind Belinda's neck he spread,
As o'er the fragrant steams she bends her head.
Swift to the lock a thousand sprites repair,
A thousand wings, by turns, blow back the hair;
And thrice they twitch'd the diamond in her ear;
Thrice she look'd back, and thrice the foe drew near.
Just in that instant, anxious Ariel sought
The close recesses of the virgin's thought;
As on the nosegay in her breast reclined,
He watch'd the ideas rising in her mind,

Sudden he view'd, in spite of all her art,
An earthly lover lurking at her heart.
Amazed, confused, he found his power expired,
Resign'd to fate, and with a sigh retired.

The Peer now spreads the glittering forfex wide,
To inclose the lock; now joins it to divide.
Even then, before the fatal engine closed,
A wretched Sylph too fondly interposed;
Fate urged the shears, and cut the Sylph in twain,
(But airy substance soon unites again)
The meeting points the sacred hair dissever
From the fair head, for ever, and for ever!

Then flash'd the living lightning from her eyes,
And screams of horror rend the affrighted skies.
Not louder shrieks to pitying heaven are cast,
When husbands, or when lapdogs breathe their last;
Or when rich China vessels, fallen from high,
In glittering dust and painted fragments lie!

'Let wreaths of triumph now my temples twine,
(The victor cried) the glorious prize is mine!
While fish in streams, or birds delight in air,
Or in a coach-and-six the British fair,
As long as Atalantis shall be read,
Or the small pillow grace a lady's bed,
While visits shall be paid on solemn days,
When numerous wax-lights in bright order blaze,
While nymphs take treats, or assignations give,
So long my honour, name, and praise shall live!'

What Time would spare, from steel receives its date,
And monuments, like men, submit to fate!
Steel could the labour of the gods destroy,
And strike to dust the imperial towers of Troy;
Steel could the works of mortal pride confound,
And hew triumphal arches to the ground.
What wonder then, fair nymph! thy hairs should feel,
The conquering force of unresisted steel?

CANTO IV

But anxious cares the pensive nymph oppress'd,
And secret passions labour'd in her breast.
Not youthful kings in battle seized alive,

Not scornful virgins who their charms survive,
Not ardent lovers robb'd of all their bliss,
Not ancient ladies when refused a kiss,
Not tyrants fierce that unrepenting die,
Not Cynthia when her manteau's pinn'd awry,
E'er felt such rage, resentment, and despair,
As thou, sad virgin! for thy ravish'd hair.

For, that sad moment, when the Sylphs withdrew,
And Ariel weeping from Belinda flew,
Umbriel, a dusky, melancholy sprite,
As ever sullied the fair face of light,
Down to the central earth, his proper scene,
Repair'd, to search the gloomy cave of Spleen.

Swift on his sooty pinions flits the Gnome,
And in a vapour reach'd the dismal dome.
No cheerful breeze this sullen region knows,
The dreaded east is all the wind that blows;
Here in a grotto, shelter'd close from air,
And screened in shades from day's detested glare,
She sighs for ever on her pensive bed,
Pain at her side, and Megrim at her head.

Two handmaids wait the throne: alike in place,
But differing far in figure and in face.
Here stood Ill-nature like an ancient maid,
Her wrinkled form in black and white array'd;
With store of prayers for mornings, nights, and noons
Her hand is fill'd; her bosom with lampoons.

There Affectation, with a sickly mien,
Shows in her cheek the roses of eighteen;
Practised to lisp, and hang the head aside,
Faints into airs, and languishes with pride;
On the rich quilt sinks with becoming woe,
Wrapp'd in a gown, for sickness, and for show.
The fair ones feel such maladies as these,
When each new night-dress gives a new disease.

A constant vapour o'er the palace flies,
Strange phantoms rising as the mists arise;
Dreadful, as hermits' dreams in haunted shades,
Or bright, as visions of expiring maids.
Now glaring fiends, and snakes on rolling spires,
Pale spectres, gaping tombs, and purple fires:
Now lakes of liquid gold, Elysian scenes,
And crystal domes, and angels in machines.

Unnumber'd throngs on every side are seen
Of bodies changed to various forms by Spleen.
Here living teapots stand, one arm held out,
One bent; the handle this, and that the spout:
A pipkin there, like Homer's tripod walks;
Here sighs a jar, and there a goose-pie talks;
Men prove with child, as powerful fancy works,
And maids turn'd bottles, call aloud for corks.

Safe pass'd the Gnome through this fantastic band,
A branch of healing spleenwort in his hand.
Then thus address'd the power—'Hail, wayward Queen!
Who rule the sex to fifty from fifteen:
Parent of vapours and of female wit,
Who give the hysteric, or poetic fit,
On various tempers act by various ways,
Make some take physic, others scribble plays;
Who cause the proud their visits to delay,
And send the godly in a pet to pray;
A nymph there is, that all thy power disdains,
And thousands more in equal mirth maintains.
But oh! if e'er thy Gnome could spoil a grace,
Or raise a pimple on a beauteous face,
Like citron-waters matrons' cheeks inflame,
Or change complexions at a losing game;
If e'er with airy horns I planted heads,
Or rumpled petticoats, or tumbled beds,
Or caused suspicion when no soul was rude,
Or discomposed the head-dress of a prude,
Or e'er to costive lapdog gave disease,
Which not the tears of brightest eyes could ease:
Hear me, and touch Belinda with chagrin,
That single act gives half the world the spleen.'

The goddess with a discontented air
Seems to reject him, though she grants his prayer.
A wondrous bag with both her hands she binds,
Like that where once Ulysses held the winds;
There she collects the force of female lungs,
Sighs, sobs, and passions, and the war of tongues.
A vial next she fills with fainting fears,
Soft sorrows, melting griefs, and flowing tears.
The Gnome rejoicing bears her gifts away,
Spreads his black wings, and slowly mounts to day.

Sunk in Thalestris' arms the nymph he found,
Her eyes dejected and her hair unbound.
Full o'er their heads the swelling bag he rent,

And all the furies issued at the vent.
Belinda burns with more than mortal ire,
And fierce Thalestris fans the rising fire.
'O wretched maid!' she spread her hands, and cried,
(While Hampton's echoes 'wretched maid!' replied)
'Was it for this you took such constant care
The bodkin, comb, and essence to prepare?
For this your locks in paper durance bound,
For this with torturing irons wreath'd around?
For this with fillets strain'd your tender head,
And bravely bore the double loads of lead?
Gods! shall the ravisher display your hair,
While the fops envy, and the ladies stare?
Honour forbid! at whose unrivall'd shrine
Ease, pleasure, virtue, all our sex resign.
Methinks already I your tears survey,
Already hear the horrid things they say,
Already see you a degraded toast,
And all your honour in a whisper lost!
How shall I, then, your helpless fame defend?
'Twill then be infamy to seem your friend!
And shall this prize, the inestimable prize,
Exposed through crystal to the gazing eyes,
And heighten'd by the diamond's circling rays,
On that rapacious hand for ever blaze?
Sooner shall grass in Hyde-park Circus grow,
And wits take lodgings in the sound of Bow;
Sooner let earth, air, sea to chaos fall,
Men, monkeys, lapdogs, parrots, perish all!'

She said; then raging to Sir Plume repairs,
And bids her beau demand the precious hairs:
(Sir Plume of amber snuff-box justly vain,
And the nice conduct of a clouded cane.)
With earnest eyes, and round, unthinking face,
He first the snuff-box open'd, then the case,
And thus broke out—'My Lord, why, what the devil?
Z—ds! damn the lock! 'fore Gad, you must be civil!
Plague on't! 'tis past a jest—nay, prithee, pox!
Give her the hair'—he spoke, and rapp'd his box.

'It grieves me much' (replied the Peer again)
Who speaks so well should ever speak in vain;
'But by this lock, this sacred lock I swear,
(Which never more shall join its parted hair;
Which never more its honours shall renew,
Clipp'd from the lovely head where late it grew)
That while my nostrils draw the vital air,

This hand, which won it, shall for ever wear.'
He spoke, and, speaking, in proud triumph spread
The long-contended honours of her head.

But Umbriel, hateful Gnome! forbears not so;
He breaks the vial whence the sorrows flow.
Then see! the nymph in beauteous grief appears,
Her eyes half-languishing, half-drown'd in tears;
On her heaved bosom hung her drooping head,
Which, with a sigh, she raised; and thus she said:

'For ever cursed be this detested day,
Which snatch'd my best, my favourite curl away!
Happy! ah, ten times happy had I been,
If Hampton Court these eyes had never seen!
Yet am not I the first mistaken maid,
By love of courts to numerous ills betray'd.
Oh, had I rather unadmired remain'd
In some lone isle, or distant northern land;
Where the gilt chariot never marks the way,
Where none learn ombre, none e'er taste bohea!
There kept my charms conceal'd from mortal eye,
Like roses that in deserts bloom and die.
What moved my mind with youthful lords to roam?
Oh, had I stay'd, and said my prayers at home!
'Twas this the morning omens seem'd to tell:
Thrice from my trembling hand the patch-box fell;
The tottering china shook without a wind,
Nay, Poll sat mute, and Shock was most unkind!
A Sylph too warn'd me of the threats of Fate,
In mystic visions, now believed too late.
See the poor remnants of these slighted hairs!
My hands shall rend what ev'n thy rapine spares:
These in two sable ringlets taught to break,
Once gave new beauties to the snowy neck;
The sister-lock now sits uncouth, alone,
And in its fellow's fate foresees its own;
Uncurl'd it hangs, the fatal shears demands,
And tempts, once more, thy sacrilegious hands.
Oh hadst thou, cruel! been content to seize
Hairs less in sight, or any hairs but these!'

CANTO V

She said: the pitying audience melt in tears;
But Fate and Jove had stopp'd the Baron's ears.

In vain Thalestris with reproach assails,
For who can move when fair Belinda fails?
Not half so fix'd the Trojan could remain,
While Anna begg'd and Dido raged in vain.
Then grave Clarissa graceful waved her fan;
Silence ensued, and thus the nymph began:

'Say, why are beauties praised and honour'd most,
The wise man's passion, and the vain man's toast?
Why deck'd with all that land and sea afford?
Why angels call'd, and angel-like adored?
Why round our coaches crowd the white-gloved beaux?
Why bows the side-box from its inmost rows?
How vain are all these glories, all our pains,
Unless good sense preserve what beauty gains:
That men may say, when we the front-box grace,
Behold the first in virtue as in face!
Oh! if to dance all night, and dress all day,
Charm'd the small-pox, or chased old-age away;
Who would not scorn what housewife's cares produce,
Or who would learn one earthly thing of use?
To patch, nay ogle, might become a saint,
Nor could it, sure, be such a sin to paint.
But since, alas! frail beauty must decay,
Curl'd or uncurl'd, since locks will turn to gray;
Since painted, or not painted, all shall fade,
And she who scorns a man, must die a maid;
What then remains, but well our power to use,
And keep good-humour still, whate'er we lose?
And trust me, dear! good-humour can prevail,
When airs, and flights, and screams, and scolding fail.
Beauties in vain their pretty eyes may roll;
Charms strike the sight, but merit wins the soul.'

So spoke the dame, but no applause ensued;
Belinda frown'd, Thalestris call'd her prude.
'To arms, to arms!' the fierce virago cries,
And swift as lightning to the combat flies.
All side in parties, and begin the attack;
Fans clap, silks rustle, and tough whalebones crack;
Heroes' and heroines' shouts confusedly rise,
And bass and treble voices strike the skies.
No common weapons in their hands are found,
Like gods they fight, nor dread a mortal wound.

So when bold Homer makes the gods engage,
And heavenly breasts with human passions rage;
'Gainst Pallas, Mars; Latona, Hermes arms,

And all Olympus rings with loud alarms:
Jove's thunder roars, heaven trembles all around,
Blue Neptune storms, the bellowing deeps resound:
Earth shakes her nodding towers, the ground gives way,
And the pale ghosts start at the flash of day!

Triumphant Umbriel on a sconce's height
Clapp'd his glad wings, and sat to view the fight;
Propp'd on their bodkin spears, the sprites survey
The growing combat, or assist the fray.

While through the press enraged Thalestris flies,
And scatters death around from both her eyes,
A beau and witling perish'd in the throng,
One died in metaphor, and one in song.
'O cruel nymph! a living death I bear,'
Cried Dapperwit, and sunk beside his chair.
A mournful glance Sir Fopling upwards cast,
'Those eyes are made so killing!'—was his last.
Thus on Maeander's flowery margin lies
The expiring swan, and as he sings he dies.

When bold Sir Plume had drawn Clarissa down,
Chloe stepped in, and kill'd him with a frown;
She smiled to see the doughty hero slain,
But, at her smile, the beau revived again.

Now Jove suspends his golden scales in air,
Weighs the men's wits against the lady's hair;
The doubtful beam long nods from side to side;
At length the wits mount up, the hairs subside.

See fierce Belinda on the Baron flies,
With more than usual lightning in her eyes:
Nor fear'd the chief th' unequal fight to try,
Who sought no more than on his foe to die.
But this bold lord, with manly strength endued,
She with one finger and a thumb subdued:
Just where the breath of life his nostrils drew,
A charge of snuff the wily virgin threw;
The Gnomes direct, to every atom just,
The pungent grains of titillating dust.
Sudden, with starting tears each eye o'erflows,
And the high dome re-echoes to his nose.
'Now meet thy fate!' incensed Belinda cried,
And drew a deadly bodkin from her side,
(The same, his ancient personage to deck,
Her great-great-grandsire wore about his neck,

In three seal-rings; which after, melted down,
Form'd a vast buckle for his widow's gown:
Her infant grandame's whistle next it grew,
The bells she jingled, and the whistle blew;
Then in a bodkin graced her mother's hairs,
Which long she wore, and now Belinda wears.)
'Boast not my fall,' (he cried) 'insulting foe!
Thou by some other shalt be laid as low.
Nor think, to die dejects my lofty mind:
All that I dread is leaving you behind!
Rather than so, ah! let me still survive,
And burn in Cupid's flames,—but burn alive.'

'Restore the lock!' she cries; and all around
'Restore the lock!' the vaulted roofs rebound.
Not fierce Othello in so loud a strain
Roar'd for the handkerchief that caused his pain.
But see how oft ambitious aims are cross'd,
And chiefs contend till all the prize is lost!
The lock, obtain'd with guilt, and kept with pain,
In every place is sought, but sought in vain:
With such a prize no mortal must be blest,
So Heaven decrees! with Heaven who can contest?

Some thought it mounted to the lunar sphere,
Since all things lost on earth are treasured there.
There heroes' wits are kept in ponderous vases,
And beaux' in snuff-boxes and tweezer-cases.
There broken vows, and death-bed alms are found,
And lovers' hearts with ends of ribbon bound,
The courtier's promises, and sick man's prayers,
The smiles of harlots, and the tears of heirs,
Cages for gnats, and chains to yoke a flea,
Dried butterflies, and tomes of casuistry.

But trust the Muse—she saw it upward rise,
Though mark'd by none but quick, poetic eyes:
(So Rome's great founder to the heavens withdrew,
To Proculus alone confess'd in view)
A sudden star, it shot through liquid air,
And drew behind a radiant trail of hair.
Not Berenice's locks first rose so bright,
The heaven's bespangling with dishevell'd light.
The Sylphs behold it kindling as it flies,
And, pleased, pursue its progress through the skies.

This the beau-monde shall from the Mall survey,
And hail with music its propitious ray.

This the bless'd lover shall for Venus take,
And send up vows from Rosamonda's lake.
This Partridge soon shall view in cloudless skies,
When next he looks through Galileo's eyes;
And hence th' egregious wizard shall foredoom
The fate of Louis, and the fall of Rome.

Then cease, bright nymph! to mourn thy ravish'd hair,
Which adds new glory to the shining sphere!
Not all the tresses that fair head can boast,
Shall draw such envy as the lock you lost.
For, after all the murders of your eye,
When, after millions slain, yourself shall die;
When those fair suns shall set, as set they must,
And all those tresses shall be laid in dust,
This lock the Muse shall consecrate to fame,
And 'midst the stars inscribe Belinda's name.

PASTORALS

WITH A DISCOURSE ON PASTORAL POETRY

Rura mihi et rigui placeant in vallibus amnes,
Flumina amem, sylvasque, inglorius!

VIRG.

There are not, I believe, a greater number of any sort of verses than of those which are called Pastorals; nor a smaller, than of those which are truly so. It therefore seems necessary to give some account of this kind of poem; and it is my design to comprise in this short paper the substance of those numerous dissertations the critics have made on the subject, without omitting any of their rules in my own favour. You will also find some points reconciled, about which they seem to differ, and a few remarks which, I think, have escaped their observation.

The original of poetry is ascribed to that age which succeeded the creation of the world: and as the keeping of flocks seems to have been the first employment of mankind, the most ancient sort of poetry was probably pastoral. It is natural to imagine, that the leisure of those ancient shepherds admitting and inviting some diversion, none was so proper to that solitary and sedentary life as singing; and that in their songs they took occasion to celebrate their own felicity. From hence a poem was invented, and afterwards improved to a perfect image of that happy time; which, by giving us an esteem for the virtues of a former age, might recommend them to the present. And since the life of shepherds was attended with more tranquility than any other rural employment, the poets chose to introduce their persons, from whom it received the name of "pastoral."

A pastoral is an imitation of the action of a shepherd, or one considered under that character. The form of this imitation is dramatic, or narrative, or mixed of both; the fable simple, the manners not too polite nor too rustic: the thoughts are plain, yet admit a little quickness and passion, but that short and flowing: the expression humble, yet as pure as the language will afford; neat, but not florid; easy and yet lively. In short, the fable, manners, thoughts, and expressions are full of the greatest simplicity in nature.

The complete character of this poem consists in simplicity, brevity, and delicacy; the two first of which render an eclogue natural, and the last delightful.

If we would copy nature, it may be useful to take this idea along with us, that pastoral is an image of what they call the Golden Age. So that we are not to describe our shepherds as shepherds at this day really are, but as they may be conceived then to have been, when the best of men followed the employment. To carry this resemblance yet further, it would not be amiss to give these shepherds some skill in astronomy, as far as it may be useful to that sort of life. And an air of piety to the gods should shine through the poem, which so visibly appears in all the works of antiquity: and it ought to preserve some relish of the old way of writing; the connexion should be loose, the narrations and descriptions short, and the periods concise. Yet it is not sufficient, that the sentences only be brief, the whole eclogue should be so too. For we cannot suppose poetry in those days to have been the business of men, but their recreation at vacant hours.

But with respect to the present age, nothing more conduces to make these composures natural than when some knowledge in rural affairs is discovered. This may be made to appear rather done by chance than on design, and sometimes is best shown by inference; lest by too much study to seem natural, we destroy that easy simplicity from whence arises the delight. For what is inviting in this sort of poetry, proceeds not so much from the idea of that business, as of the tranquility of a country life.

We must therefore use some illusion to render a pastoral delightful; and this consists in exposing the best side only of a shepherd's life, and in concealing its miseries. Nor is it enough to introduce shepherds discoursing together in a natural way; but a regard must be had to the subject—that it contain some particular beauty in itself, and that it be different in every eclogue. Besides, in each of them a designed scene or prospect is to be presented to our view, which should likewise have its variety. This variety is obtained in a great degree by frequent comparisons, drawn from the most agreeable objects of the country; by interrogations to things inanimate; by beautiful digressions, but those short; sometimes by insisting a little on circumstances; and lastly, by elegant turns on the words, which render the numbers extremely sweet and pleasing. As for the numbers themselves, though they are properly of the heroic measure, they should be the smoothest, the most easy and flowing imaginable.

It is by rules like these that we ought to judge of pastorals. And since the instructions given for any art are to be delivered as that art is in perfection, they must of necessity be derived from those in whom it is acknowledged so to be. It is therefore from the practice of Theocritus and Virgil (the only undisputed authors of pastoral) that the critics have drawn the foregoing notions concerning it.

Theocritus excels all others in nature and simplicity. The subjects of his 'Idyllia' are purely pastoral; but he is not so exact in his persons, having introduced reapers and fishermen as well as shepherds. He is apt to be too long in his descriptions, of which that of the cup in the first pastoral is a remarkable instance. In the manners he seems a little defective, for his swains are sometimes abusive and immodest, and perhaps too much inclining to rusticity; for instance, in his fourth and fifth 'Idyllia.' But 'tis enough that all others learnt their excellencies from him, and that his dialect alone has a secret charm in it, which no other could ever attain.

Virgil, who copies Theocritus, refines upon his original: and in all points where judgment is principally concerned, he is much superior to his master.

Though some of his subjects are not pastoral in themselves, but only seem to be such, they have a wonderful variety in them, which the Greek was a stranger to. He exceeds him in regularity and brevity, and falls short of him in nothing but simplicity and propriety of style; the first of which perhaps was the fault of his age, and the last of his language.

Among the moderns, their success has been greatest who have most endeavoured to make these ancients their pattern. The most considerable genius appears in the famous Tasso, and our Spenser. Tasso in his 'Aminta' has as far excelled all the pastoral writers, as in his 'Gierusalemme' he has outdone the epic poets of his country. But as this piece seems to have been the original of a new sort of poem— the pastoral comedy—in Italy, it cannot so well be considered as a copy of the ancients. Spenser's Calendar, in Mr Dryden's opinion, is the most complete work of this kind which any nation has produced ever since the time of Virgil. Not but that he may be thought imperfect in some few points. His Eclogues are somewhat too long, if we compare them with the ancients. He is sometimes too allegorical, and treats of matters of religion in a pastoral style, as the Mantuan had done before him. He has employed the lyric measure, which is contrary to the practice of the old poets. His stanza is not still the same, nor always well chosen. This last may be the reason his expression is sometimes not concise enough: for the Tetrastic has obliged him to extend his sense to the length of four lines, which would have been more closely confined in the couplet.

In the manners, thoughts, and characters, he comes near to Theocritus himself; though, notwithstanding all the care he has taken, he is certainly inferior in his dialect: for the Doric had its beauty and propriety in the time of Theocritus; it was used in part of Greece, and frequent in the mouths of many of the greatest persons: whereas the old English and country phrases of Spenser were either entirely obsolete, or spoken only by people of the lowest condition. As there is a difference betwixt simplicity and rusticity, so the expression of simple thoughts should be plain, but not clownish. The addition he has made of a Calendar to his Eclogues, is very beautiful; since by this, besides the general moral of innocence and simplicity, which is common to other authors of pastoral, he has one peculiar to himself—he compares human life to the several seasons, and at once exposes to his readers a view of the great and little worlds, in their various changes and aspects. Yet the scrupulous division of his pastorals into months has obliged him either to repeat the same description, in other words, for three months together; or, when it was exhausted before, entirely to omit it: whence it comes to pass that some of his Eclogues (as the sixth, eighth, and tenth, for example) have nothing but their titles to distinguish them. The reason is evident—because the year has not that variety in it to furnish every month with a particular description, as it may every season.

Of the following eclogues I shall only say, that these four comprehend all the subjects which the critics upon Theocritus and Virgil will allow to be fit for pastoral: that they have as much variety of description, in respect of the several seasons, as Spenser's: that, in order to add to this variety, the several times of the day are observed, the rural employments in each season or time of day, and the rural scenes or places proper to such employments; not without some regard to the several ages of man, and the different passions proper to each age.

But after all, if they have any merit, it is to be attributed to some good old authors, whose works as I had leisure to study, so I hope I have not wanted care to imitate.

SPRING.

THE FIRST PASTORAL, OR DAMON.

TO SIR WILLIAM TRUMBULL.

First in these fields I try the sylvan strains,
Nor blush to sport on Windsor's blissful plains:
Fair Thames, flow gently from thy sacred spring,
While on thy banks Sicilian Muses sing;
Let vernal airs through trembling osiers play,
And Albion's cliffs resound the rural lay.

You that, too wise for pride, too good for power,
Enjoy the glory to be great no more,
And, carrying with you all the world can boast,
To all the world illustriously are lost!
Oh, let my Muse her slender reed inspire,
Till in your native shades you tune the lyre:
So when the nightingale to rest removes,
The thrush may chant to the forsaken groves,
But, charm'd to silence, listens while she sings,
And all the aërial audience clap their wings.

Soon as the flocks shook off the nightly dews,
Two swains, whom Love kept wakeful, and the Muse,
Pour'd o'er the whitening vale their fleecy care,
Fresh as the morn, and as the season fair:
The dawn now blushing on the mountain's side,
Thus Daphnis spoke, and Strephou thus replied.

DAPHNIS.
Hear how the birds, on every bloomy spray,
With joyous music wake the dawning day!
Why sit we mute when early linnets sing,
When warbling Philomel salutes the spring?
Why sit we sad, when Phosphor shines so clear,
And lavish Nature paints the purple year?

STREPHON.
Sing then, and Damon shall attend the strain,
While yon slow oxen turn the furrow'd plain.
Here the bright crocus and blue violet glow;

Here western winds on breathing roses blow.
I'll stake yon lamb, that near the fountain plays,
And from the brink his dancing shade surveys.

DAPHNIS.
And I this bowl, where wanton ivy twines,
And swelling clusters bend the curling vines:
Four Figures rising from the work appear,
The various Seasons of the rolling year;
And what is that, which binds the radiant sky,
Where twelve fair signs in beauteous order lie?

DAMON.
Then sing by turns, by turns the Muses sing;
Now hawthorns blossom, now the daisies spring;
Now leaves the trees, and flowers adorn the ground:
Begin, the vales shall every note rebound.

STREPHON.
Inspire me, Phoebus, in my Delia's praise,
With Waller's strains, or Granville's moving lays!
A milk-white bull shall at your altars stand,
That threats a fight, and spurns the rising sand.

DAPHNIS.
O Love! for Sylvia let me gain the prize,
And make my tongue victorious as her eyes;
No lambs or sheep for victims I'll impart,
Thy victim, Love, shall be the shepherd's heart.

STREPHON.
Me gentle Delia beckons from the plain,
Then hid in shades, eludes her eager swain;
But feigns a laugh, to see me search around,
And by that laugh the willing fair is found.

DAPHNIS.
The sprightly Sylvia trips along the green,
She runs, but hopes she does not run unseen;
While a kind glance at her pursuer flies,
How much at variance are her feet and eyes!

STREPHON.
O'er golden sands let rich Pactolus flow,
And trees weep amber on the banks of Po;
Blest Thames's shores the brightest beauties yield,
Feed here, my lambs, I'll seek no distant field.

DAPHNIS.
Celestial Venus haunts Idalia's groves;
Diana Cynthus, Ceres Hybla loves;
If Windsor-shades delight the matchless maid,
Cynthus and Hybla yield to Windsor-shade.

STREPHON.
All nature mourns, the skies relent in showers,
Hush'd are the birds, and closed the drooping flowers;
If Delia smile, the flowers begin to spring,
The skies to brighten, and the birds to sing.

DAPHNIS.
All nature laughs, the groves are fresh and fair,
The sun's mild lustre warms the vital air;
If Sylvia smiles, new glories gild the shore,
And vanquish'd Nature seems to charm no more.

STREPHON.
In spring the fields, in autumn hills I love,
At morn the plains, at noon the shady grove,
But Delia always; absent from her sight,
Nor plains at morn, nor groves at noon delight.

DAPHNIS.
Sylvia's like autumn ripe, yet mild as May,
More bright than noon, yet fresh as early day;
Even spring displeases, when she shines not here;
But, blest with her, 'tis spring throughout the year.

STREPHON.
Say, Daphnis, say, in what glad soil appears,
A wondrous tree that sacred monarchs bears?
Tell me but this, and I'll disclaim the prize,
And give the conquest to thy Sylvia's eyes.

DAPHNIS.
Nay, tell me first, in what more happy fields
The thistle springs, to which the lily yields?
And then a nobler prize I will resign;
For Sylvia, charming Sylvia shall be thine.

DAMON.
Cease to contend, for, Daphnis, I decree,
The bowl to Strephon, and the lamb to thee:
Blest swains, whose nymphs in every grace excel;
Blest nymphs, whose swains those graces sing so well!
Now rise, and haste to yonder woodbine bowers,

A soft retreat from sudden vernal showers;
The turf with rural dainties shall be crown'd.
While opening blooms diffuse their sweets around.
For see! the gath'ring flocks to shelter tend,
And from the Pleiads fruitful showers descend.

SUMMER,

THE SECOND PASTORAL, OR ALEXIS.

TO DR GARTH.

A shepherd's boy (he seeks no better name)
Led forth his flocks along the silver Thame,
Where dancing sunbeams on the waters play'd,
And verdant alders form'd a quivering shade.
Soft as he mourn'd, the streams forgot to flow,
The flocks around a dumb compassion show:
The Naïads wept in every watery bower,
And Jove consented in a silent shower.

Accept, O Garth the Muse's early lays,
That adds this wreath of ivy to thy bays;
Hear what from love unpractised hearts endure:
From love, the sole disease thou canst not cure.

Ye shady beeches, and ye cooling streams,
Defence from Phoebus', not from Cupid's beams,
To you I mourn, nor to the deaf I sing,
'The woods shall answer, and their echo ring.'
The hills and rocks attend my doleful lay;
Why art thou prouder and more hard than they?
The bleating sheep with my complaints agree,
They parch'd with heat, and I inflamed by thee.
The sultry Sirius burns the thirsty plains,
While in thy heart eternal winter reigns.

Where stray ye, Muses, in what lawn or grove,
While your Alexis pines in hopeless love?
In those fair fields where sacred Isis glides,
Or else where Cam his winding vales divides?
As in the crystal spring I view my face,
Fresh rising blushes paint the watery glass;
But since those graces please thy eyes no more,
I shun the fountains which I sought before.
Once I was skill'd in every herb that grew,

And every plant that drinks the morning dew;
Ah, wretched shepherd, what avails thy art,
To cure thy lambs, but not to heal thy heart!
Let other swains attend the rural care,
Feed fairer flocks, or richer fleeces shear:
But nigh yon mountain let me tune my lays,
Embrace my love, and bind my brows with bays.
That flute is mine which Colin's tuneful breath
Inspired when living, and bequeath'd in death;
He said, 'Alexis, take this pipe—the same
That taught the groves my Rosalinda's name:'
But now the reeds shall hang on yonder tree,
For ever silent, since despised by thee.
Oh! were I made by some transforming power
The captive bird that sings within thy bower!
Then might my voice thy listening ears employ,
And I those kisses he receives, enjoy.

And yet my numbers please the rural throng,
Rough Satyrs dance, and Pan applauds the song:
The Nymphs, forsaking every cave and spring,
Their early fruit, and milk-white turtles bring;
Each amorous nymph prefers her gifts in vain.
On you their gifts are all bestow'd again.
For you the swains the fairest flowers design,
And in one garland all their beauties join;
Accept the wreath which you deserve alone,
In whom all beauties are comprised in one.

See what delights in sylvan scenes appear!
Descending gods have found Elysium here.
In woods bright Venus with Adonis stray'd,
And chaste Diana haunts the forest shade.
Come, lovely nymph, and bless the silent hours,
When swains from shearing seek their nightly bowers,
When weary reapers quit the sultry field,
And crown'd with corn their thanks to Ceres yield;
This harmless grove no lurking viper hides,
But in my breast the serpent love abides.
Here bees from blossoms sip the rosy dew,
But your Alexis knows no sweets but you.
Oh, deign to visit our forsaken seats,
The mossy fountains, and the green retreats!
Where'er you walk, cool gales shall fan the glade,
Trees, where you sit, shall crowd into a shade:
Where'er you tread, the blushing flowers shall rise,
And all things flourish where you turn your eyes.
Oh, how I long with you to pass my days,

Invoke the Muses, and resound your praise!
Your praise the birds shall chant in every grove,
And winds shall waft it to the Powers above.
But would you sing, and rival Orpheus' strain,
The wondering forests soon should dance again,
The moving mountains hear the powerful call,
And headlong streams hang listening in their fall!

But see, the shepherds shun the noonday heat,
The lowing herds to murmuring brooks retreat,
To closer shades the panting flocks remove;
Ye gods! and is there no relief for love?
But soon the sun with milder rays descends
To the cool ocean, where his journey ends:
On me Love's fiercer flames for ever prey,
By night he scorches, as he burns by day.

AUTUMN.

THE THIRD PASTORAL, Or HYLAS AND ÆGON.

TO MR WYCHERLEY

Beneath the shade a spreading beech displays,
Hylas and Ægon sung their rural lays;
This mourn'd a faithless, that an absent love.
And Delia's name and Doris' fill'd the grove.
Ye Mantuan nymphs, your sacred succour bring;
Hylas and Ægon's rural lays I sing.

Thou, whom the Nine with Plautus' wit inspire,
The art of Terence, and Menander's fire;
Whose sense instructs us, and whose humour charms,
Whose judgment sways us, and whose spirit warms!
Oh, skill'd in Nature! see the hearts of swains,
Their artless passions, and their tender pains.

Now setting Phoebus shone serenely bright,
And fleecy clouds were streak'd with purple light;
When tuneful Hylas, with melodious moan,
Taught rocks to weep, and made the mountains groan.

Go, gentle gales, and bear my sighs away!
To Delia's ear the tender notes convey.
As some sad turtle his lost love deplores,
And with deep murmurs fills the sounding shores,

Thus, far from Delia, to the winds I mourn,
Alike unheard, unpitied, and forlorn.

Go, gentle gales, and bear my sighs along!
For her, the feather'd choirs neglect their song:
For her, the limes their pleasing shades deny;
For her, the lilies hang their heads and die.
Ye flowers that droop, forsaken by the spring,
Ye birds that, left by summer, cease to sing,
Ye trees that fade when autumn-heats remove,
Say, is not absence death to those who love?

Go, gentle gales, and bear my sighs away!
Cursed be the fields that cause my Delia's stay;
Fade every blossom, wither every tree,
Die every flower, and perish all but she.

What have I said? Where'er my Delia flies,
Let spring attend, and sudden flowers arise;
Let opening roses knotted oaks adorn,
And liquid amber drop from every thorn.

Go, gentle gales, and bear my sighs along!
The birds shall cease to tune their evening song,
The winds to breathe, the waving woods to move,
And streams to murmur, ere I cease to love.
Not bubbling fountains to the thirsty swain,
Not balmy sleep to labourers faint with pain,
Not showers to larks, or sunshine to the bee,
Are half so charming as thy sight to me.
Go, gentle gales, and bear my sighs away!
Come, Delia, come; ah, why this long delay?
Through rocks and caves the name of Delia sounds,
Delia, each care and echoing rock rebounds.
Ye Powers, what pleasing frenzy soothes my mind!
Do lovers dream, or is my Delia kind?
She comes, my Delia comes!—Now cease, my lay,
And cease, ye gales, to bear my sighs away!

Next Ægon sung, while Windsor groves admired;
Rehearse, ye Muses, what yourselves inspired.

Resound, ye hills, resound my mournful strain!
Of perjured Doris, dying I complain:
Here where the mountains, lessening as they rise,
Lose the low vales, and steal into the skies:
While labouring oxen, spent with toil and heat,
In their loose traces from the field retreat:

While curling smokes from village-tops are seen,
And the fleet shades glide o'er the dusky green.

Resound, ye hills, resound my mournful lay!
Beneath yon poplar oft we pass'd the day:
Oft on the rind I carved her amorous vows,
While she with garlands hung the bending boughs:
The garlands fade, the vows are worn away;
So dies her love, and so my hopes decay.

Resound, ye hills, resound my mournful strain!
Now bright Arcturus glads the teeming grain,
Now golden fruits on loaded branches shine,
And grateful clusters swell with floods of wine;
Now blushing berries paint the yellow grove;
Just gods! shall all things yield returns but love?

Resound, ye hills, resound my mournful lay!
The shepherds cry, 'Thy flocks are left a prey'—
Ah! what avails it me, the flocks to keep,
Who lost my heart—while I preserved my sheep.
Pan came, and ask'd, what magic caused my smart,
Or what ill eyes malignant glances dart?
What eyes but hers, alas, have power to move?
And is there magic but what dwells in love?

Resound, ye hills, resound my mournful strains!
I'll fly from shepherds, flocks, and flowery plains.
From shepherds, flocks, and plains, I may remove,
Forsake mankind, and all the world—but Love!
I know thee, Love! on foreign mountains bred,
Wolves gave thee suck, and savage tigers fed.
Thou wert from Etna's burning entrails torn,
Got by fierce whirlwinds, and in thunder born!

Resound, ye hills, resound my mournful lay!
Farewell, ye woods; adieu, the light of day!
One leap from yonder cliff shall end my pains;
No more, ye hills, no more resound my strains!

Thus sung the shepherds till the approach of night,
The skies yet blushing with departing light,
When falling dews with spangles deck'd the glade,
And the low sun had lengthen'd every shade.

WINTER.

THE FOURTH PASTORAL, OR DAPHNE.

TO THE MEMORY OF MRS TEMPEST

LYCIDAS.
Thyrsis, the music of that murmuring spring
Is not so mournful as the strains you sing;
Nor rivers winding through the vales below,
So sweetly warble, or so smoothly flow.
Now sleeping flocks on their soft fleeces lie,
The moon, serene in glory, mounts the sky,
While silent birds forget their tuneful lays,
Oh sing of Daphne's fate, and Daphne's praise!

THYRSIS.
Behold the groves that shine with silver frost,
Their beauty wither'd, and their verdure lost.
Here shall I try the sweet Alexis' strain,
That call'd the listening Dryads to the plain?
Thames heard the numbers as he flow'd along,
And bade his willows learn the moving song.

LYCIDAS.
So may kind rains their vital moisture yield
And swell the future harvest of the field.
Begin; this charge the dying Daphne gave,
And said, 'Ye shepherds, sing around my grave!'
Sing, while beside the shaded tomb I mourn,
And with fresh bays her rural shrine adorn.

THYRSIS.
Ye gentle Muses, leave your crystal spring,
Let nymphs and sylvans cypress garlands bring;
Ye weeping Loves, the stream with myrtles hide,
And break your bows, as when Adonis died;
And with your golden darts, now useless grown,
Inscribe a verse on this relenting stone:
'Let Nature change, let Heaven and Earth deplore,
Fair Daphne's dead, and Love is now no more!'
'Tis done, and Nature's various charms decay;
See gloomy clouds obscure the cheerful day!
Now hung with pearls the dropping trees appear,
Their faded honours scatter'd on her bier.
See where, on earth, the flowery glories lie,
With her they flourish'd, and with her they die.
Ah, what avail the beauties Nature wore,

Fair Daphne's dead, and Beauty is no more!

For her the flocks refuse their verdant food,
The thirsty heifers shun the gliding flood,
The silver swans her hapless fate bemoan,
In notes more sad than when they sing their own;
In hollow caves sweet Echo silent lies,
Silent, or only to her name replies;
Her name with pleasure once she taught the shore;
Now Daphne's dead, and Pleasure is no more!

No grateful dews descend from evening skies,
Nor morning odours from the flowers arise;
No rich perfumes refresh the fruitful field,
Nor fragrant herbs their native incense yield.
The balmy zephyrs, silent since her death,
Lament the ceasing of a sweeter breath;
Th' industrious bees neglect their golden store;
Fair Daphne's dead, and Sweetness is no more!

No more the mounting larks, while Daphne sings,
Shall, listening in mid air, suspend their wings;
No more the birds shall imitate her lays,
Or, hush'd with wonder, hearken from the sprays:
No more the streams their murmurs shall forbear,
A sweeter music than their own to hear;
But tell the reeds, and tell the vocal shore,
Fair Daphne's dead, and Music is no more!

Her fate is whisper'd by the gentle breeze,
And told in sighs to all the trembling trees;
The trembling trees, in every plain and wood,
Her fate remurmur to the silver flood;
The silver flood, so lately calm, appears
Swell'd with new passion, and o'erflows with tears;
The winds and trees and floods her death deplore,
Daphne, our grief, our glory now no more!

But see! where Daphne wondering mounts on high
Above the clouds, above the starry sky!
Eternal beauties grace the shining scene,
Fields ever fresh, and groves for ever green!
There while you rest in amaranthine bowers,
Or from those meads select unfading flowers,
Behold us kindly, who your name implore,
Daphne, our goddess, and our grief no more!

LYCIDAS.

How all things listen, while thy Muse complains!
Such silence waits on Philomela's strains,
In some still evening, when the whispering breeze
Pants on the leaves, and dies upon the trees.
To thee, bright goddess, oft a lamb shall bleed,
If teeming ewes increase my fleecy breed.
While plants their shade, or flowers their odours give,
Thy name, thy honour, and thy praise shall live!

THYRSIS.
But see, Orion sheds unwholesome dews;
Arise, the pines a noxious shade diffuse;
Sharp Boreas blows, and Nature feels decay,
Time conquers all, and we must Time obey.
Adieu, ye vales, ye mountains, streams, and groves;
Adieu, ye shepherds, rural lays, and loves;
Adieu, my flocks; farewell, ye sylvan crew;
Daphne, farewell; and all the world, adieu!

Alexander Pope – A Short Biography

Alexander Pope was born in Lombard Street, London, on the 21st of May 1688—the year of the Revolution. His father was a linen-merchant, in thriving circumstances, and said to have noble blood in his veins. His mother was Edith or Editha Turner, daughter of William Turner, Esq., of York. Mr Carruthers, in his excellent Life of the Poet, mentions that there was an Alexander Pope, a clergyman, in the remote parish of Reay, in Caithness, who rode all the way to Twickenham to pay his great namesake a visit, and was presented by him with a copy of the subscription edition of the "Odyssey," in five volumes quarto, which is still preserved by his descendants. Pope's father had made about £10,000 by trade; but being a Roman Catholic, and fond of a country life, he retired from business shortly after the Revolution, at the early age of forty-six. He resided first at Kensington, and then in Binfield, in the neighbourhood of Windsor Forest. He is said to have put his money in a strong box, and to have lived on the principal. His great delight was in his garden; and both he and his wife seem to have cherished the warmest interest in their son, who was very delicate in health, and their only child. Pope's study is still preserved in Binfield; and on the lawn, a cypress-tree which he is said to have planted, is pointed out.

Pope was a premature and precocious child. His figure was deformed—his back humped—his stature short (four feet six inches)—his legs and arms disproportionably long. He was sometimes compared to a spider, and sometimes to a windmill. The only mark of genius lay in his bright and piercing eye. He was sickly in constitution, and required and received great tenderness and care. Once, when three years old, he narrowly escaped from an angry cow, but was wounded in the throat. He was remarkable as a child for his amiable temper; and from the sweetness of his voice, received the name of the Little Nightingale. His aunt gave him his first lessons in reading, and he soon became an enthusiastic lover of books; and by copying printed characters, taught himself to write. When eight years old, he was placed under the care of the family priest, one Bannister, who taught him the Latin and Greek grammars together. He was next removed to a Catholic seminary at Twyford, near Winchester; and while there, read Ogilby's "Homer" and Sandys's "Ovid" with great delight. He had not been long at this school till he wrote a severe lampoon, of two hundred lines' length, on his master—so truly was the "boy the father of the man"—for which demi-Dunciad he was severely flogged. His father, offended at this, removed him to a London school, kept by a Mr Deane. This man taught the poet nothing; but his residence in London gave him the opportunity of attending the theatres. With these he was so captivated, that he wrote a kind of play, which was acted by his schoolfellows, consisting of speeches from Ogilby's "Iliad," tacked together with verses of his own. He became acquainted with Dryden's works, and went to Wills's coffee-house to see him. He says, "Virgilium tantum vidi." Such transient meetings of literary orbs are among the most interesting passages in biography. Thus met Galileo with Milton, Milton with Dryden, Dryden with Pope, and Burns with Scott. Carruthers strikingly remarks, "Considering the perils and uncertainties of a literary life—its precarious rewards, feverish anxieties, mortifications, and disappointments, joined to the tyranny of the Tonsons and Lintots, and the malice and envy of dunces, all of which Dryden had long and bitterly experienced—the aged poet could hardly have looked at the delicate and deformed boy, whose preternatural acuteness and sensibility were seen in his dark eyes, without a feeling approaching to grief, had he known that he was to fight a battle like that under which he was himself then sinking, even though the Temple of Fame should at length open to receive him." At twelve, he wrote the "Ode to Solitude;" and shortly after, his satirical piece on Elkanah Settle, and some of his translations and imitations. His next period, he says, was in Windsor Forest, where for several years he did nothing but read the classics and indite poetry. He wrote a tragedy, a comedy, and four books of an Epic called "Alexander," all of which afterwards he committed to the flames. He translated also a portion of Statius, and Cicero "De Senectute," and "thought himself the greatest genius that ever was." His father encouraged him in his studies, and when his verses did not please him, sent him back to "new turn" them, saying, "These are not good rhymes." His principal favourites were Virgil's "Eclogues," in Latin; and in English, Spencer, Waller, and Dryden—admiring Spencer, we presume, for his luxuriant fancy, Waller for his smooth versification, and Dryden for his vigorous sense and vivid sarcasm. In the Forest, he became acquainted with Sir William Trumbull, the retired secretary of state, a man of general accomplishments, who read, rode, conversed with the youthful poet; introduced him to old Wycherley, the dramatist; and was of material service to his views. With Wycherley, who was old, doted, and excessively vain, Pope did not continue long intimate. A coldness, springing from some criticisms which the youth ventured to make on the veteran's poetry, crept in between them. Walsh of Abberley, in Worcestershire, a man of good sense and taste, became, after a perusal of the "Pastorals" in MS., a warm friend and kind adviser of Pope's, who has immortalised him in more than one of his poems. Walsh told Pope that there had never hitherto appeared in Britain a poet who was at once great and correct, and exhorted him to aim at accuracy and elegance.

When fifteen, he visited London, in order to acquire a more thorough knowledge of French and Italian. At sixteen, he wrote the "Pastorals," and a portion of "Windsor Forest," although they were not published for some time afterwards. By his incessant exertions, he now began to feel his constitution injured. He imagined himself dying, and sent farewell letters to all his friends, including the Abbé Southcot. This gentleman communicated Pope's case to Dr Ratcliffe, who gave him some medical directions; by following which, the poet recovered. He was advised to relax in his studies, and to ride daily; and he prudently followed the advice. Many years afterwards, he repaid the benevolent Abbé by procuring for him, through Sir Robert Walpole, the nomination to an abbey in Avignon. This is only one of many proofs that, notwithstanding his waspish temper, and his no small share of malice as well as vanity, there was a warm heart in our poet.

In 1707, Pope became acquainted with Michael Blount of Maple, Durham, near Reading; whose two sisters, Martha and Teresa, he has commemorated in various verses. On his connexion with these ladies, some mystery rests. Bowles has strongly and plausibly urged that it was not of the purest or most creditable order. Others have contended that it did not go further than the manners of the age sanctioned; and they say, "a much greater license in conversation and in epistolary correspondence was permitted between the sexes than in our decorous age!" We are not careful to try and settle such a delicate question—only we are inclined to suspect, that when common decency quits the words of male and female parties in their mutual communications, it is a very ample charity that can suppose it to adhere to their actions. And nowhere do we find grosser language than in some of Pope's prose epistles to the Blounts.

His "Pastorals," after having been handed about in MS., and shewn to such reputed judges as Lord Halifax, Lord Somers, Garth, Congreve, &c., were at last, in 1709, printed in the sixth volume of Tonson's "Miscellanies." Like all well-finished commonplaces, they were received with instant and universal applause. It is humiliating to contrast the reception of these empty echoes of inspiration, these agreeable centos, with that of such genuine, although faulty poems, as Keat's "Endymion," Shelley's "Queen Mab," and Wordsworth's "Lyrical Ballads." Two years later, (in 1711), a far better and more characteristic production from his pen was ushered anonymously into the world. This was the "Essay on Criticism," a work which he had first written in prose, and which discovers a ripeness of judgment, a clearness of thought, a condensation of style, and a command over the information he possesses, worthy of any age in life, and almost of any mind in time. It serves, indeed, to shew what Pope's true forte was. That lay not so much in poetry, as in the knowledge of its principles and laws, not so much in creation, as in criticism. He was no Homer or Shakspeare; but he might have been nearly as acute a judge of poetry as Aristotle, and nearly as eloquent an expounder of the rules of art and the glories of genius as Longinus.

In the same year, Pope printed "The Rape of the Lock," in a volume of Miscellanies. Lord Petre had, much in the way described by the poet, stolen a lock of Miss Belle Fermor's hair, a feat which led to an estrangement between the families. Pope set himself to reconcile them by this beautiful poem, a poem which has embalmed at once the quarrel and the reconciliation to all future time. In its first version, the machinery was awanting, the "lock" was a desert, the "rape" a natural event, the small infantry of sylphs and gnomes were slumbering uncreated in the poet's mind; but in the next edition he contrived to introduce them in a manner so easy and so exquisite, as to remind you of the variations which occur in dreams, where one wonder seems softly to slide into the bosom of another, and where beautiful and fantastic fancies grow suddenly out of realities, like the bud from the bough, or the fairy-seeming wing of the summer-cloud from the stern azure of the heavens.

A little after this, Pope became acquainted with a far greater, better, and truer man than himself, Joseph Addison. Warburton, and others, have sadly misrepresented the connexion between these two famous wits, as well as their relative intellectual positions. Addison was a more amiable and childlike person than Pope. He had much more, too, of the Christian. He was not so elaborately polished and furbished as the author of "The Rape of the Lock;" but he had, naturally, a finer and richer genius. Pope found early occasion for imagining Addison his disguised enemy. He gave him a hint of his intention to introduce the machinery into "The Rape of the Lock." Of this, Addison disapproved, and said it was a delicious little thing already—merum sal. This, Pope, and some of his friends, have attributed to jealousy; but it is obvious that Addison could not foresee the success with which the machinery was to be managed, and did foresee the difficulties connected with tinkering such an exquisite production. We may allude here to the circumstances which, at a later date, produced an estrangement between these celebrated men. When Tickell, Addison's friend, published the first book of the "Iliad," in opposition to Pope's version, Addison gave it the preference. This moved Pope's indignation, and led him to assert that it was Addison's own composition. In this conjecture he was supported by Edward Young, who had known Tickell long and intimately, and had never heard of him having written at college, as was averred, this translation. It is now, however, we believe, certain, from the MS. which still exists, that Tickell was the real author. A coldness, from this date, began between Pope and Addison. An attempt to reconcile them only made matters worse; and at last the breach was rendered irremediable by Pope's writing the famous character of his rival, afterwards inserted in the Prologue to the Satires, a portrait drawn with the perfection of polished malice and bitter sarcasm, but which seems more a caricature than a likeness. Whatever Addison's faults, his conduct to Pope did not deserve such a return. The whole passage is only one of those painful incidents which disgrace the history of letters, and prove how much spleen, ingratitude, and baseness often co-exist with the highest parts. The words of Pope are as true now as ever they were—"the life of a wit is a warfare upon earth;" and a warfare in which poisoned missiles and every variety of falsehood are still common. We may also here mention, that while the friendship of Pope and Addison lasted, the former contributed the well-known prologue to the latter's "Cato."

One of Pope's most intimate friends in his early days was Henry Cromwell—a distant relative of the great Oliver—a gentleman of fortune, gallantry, and literary taste, who became his agreeable and fascinating, but somewhat dangerous, companion. He is supposed to have initiated Pope into some of the fashionable follies of the town. At this time, Pope's popularity roused one of his most formidable foes against him. This was that Cobbett of criticism, old John Dennis, a man of strong natural powers, much learning, and a rich, coarse vein of humour; but irascible, vindictive, vain, and capricious. Pope had provoked him by an attack in his "Essay on Criticism," and the savage old man revenged himself by a running fire of fierce diatribes against that "Essay" and "The Rape of the Lock." Pope waited till Dennis had committed himself by a powerful but furious assault on Addison's "Cato" (most of which Johnson has preserved in his Life of Pope); and then, partly to court Addison, and partly to indulge his spleen at the critic, wrote a prose satire, entitled, "The Narrative of Dr Robert Norris on the Frenzy of J.D." In this, however, he overshot the mark; and Addison signified to him that he was displeased with the spirit of his narrative, an intimation which Pope keenly resented. This scornful dog would not eat the dirty pudding that was graciously flung to him; and Pope found that, without having conciliated Addison, he had made Dennis's furnace of hate against himself seven times hotter than before.

In 1712 appeared "The Messiah," "The Dying Christian to his Soul," "The Temple of Fame," and the "Elegy on the Memory of an Unfortunate Lady." Her story is still involved in mystery. Her name is said to have been Wainsbury. She was attached to a lover above her degree, some say to the Duke of Berry, whom she had met in her early youth in France. In despair of obtaining her desire, she hanged herself. It is curious, if true, that she was as deformed in person as Pope himself. Her family seems to have been noble. In 1713, he published "Windsor Forest," an "Ode on St Cecilia's Day," and several papers in the Guardian—one of them being an exquisitely ironical paper, comparing Phillip's pastorals with his own, and affecting to give them the preference—the extracts being so selected as to damage his rival's claims. This year, also, he wrote, although he did not publish, his fine epistle to Jervas, the painter. Pope was passionately fond of the art of painting, and practised it a good deal under Jervas's instructions, although he did not reach great proficiency. The prodigy has yet to be born who combines the characters of a great painter and a great poet.

About this time, Pope commenced preparations for the great work of translating Homer; and subscription-papers, accordingly, were issued. Dean Swift was now in England, and took a deep interest in the success of this undertaking, recommending it in coffee-houses, and introducing the subject and Pope's name to the leading Tories. Pope met the Dean for the first time in Berkshire, where, in one of his fits of savage disgust at the conflicting parties of the period, he had retired to the house of a clergyman, and an intimacy commenced which was only terminated by death. We have often regretted that Pope had not selected some author more suitable to his genius than Homer. Horace or Lucretius, or even Ovid, would have been more congenial. His imitations of Horace shew us what he might have made of a complete translation. What a brilliant thing a version of Lucretius, in the style of the "Essay on Man," would have been! And his "Rape of the Lock" proves that he had considerable sympathy with the elaborate fancy, although not with the meretricious graces of Ovid. But with Homer, the severely grand, the simple, the warlike, the lover and painter of all Nature's old original forms—the ocean, the mountains, and the stars—what thorough sympathy could a man have who never saw a real mountain or a battle, and whose enthusiasm for scenery was confined to purling brooks, trim gardens, artificial grottos, and the shades of Windsor Forest? Accordingly, his Homer, although a beautiful and sparkling poem, is not a satisfactory translation of the "Iliad," and still less of the "Odyssey." He has trailed along the naked lances of the Homeric lines so many flowers and leaves that you can hardly recognise them, and feel that their point is deadened and their power gone. This at least is our opinion; although many to this day continue to admire these translations, and have even said that if they are not Homer, they are something better.

The "Iliad" took him six years, and was a work which cost him much anxiety as well as labour, the more as his scholarship was far from profound. He was assisted in the undertaking by Parnell (who wrote the Life of Homer), by Broome, Jortin, and others. The first volume appeared in June 1715, and the other volumes followed at irregular intervals. He began it in 1712, his twenty-fifth year, and finished it in 1718, his thirtieth year. Previous to its appearance, his remuneration for his poems had been small, and his circumstances were embarrassed; but the result of the subscription, which amounted to £5320, 4s., rendered him independent for life.

While at Binfield, he had often visited London; and there, in the society of Howe, Garth, Parnell, and the rest, used to indulge in occasional excesses, which did his feeble constitution no good; and once, according to Colley Cibber, he narrowly escaped a serious scrape in a house of a certain description, Colley, by his own account, "helping out the tomtit for the sake of Homer!" This statement, indeed, Pope has denied; but his veracity was by no means his strongest point. After writing a "Farewell to London," he retired, in 1715, to Twickenham, along with his parents; and remained there, cultivating his garden, digging his grottos, and diversifying his walks, till the end of his days.

Some years before, he had become acquainted with Lady Mary Wortley Montague, the most brilliant woman of her age—witty, fascinating, beautiful, and accomplished—full of enterprise and spirit, too, although decidedly French in her tastes, manners, and character. Pope fell violently in love with her, and had her undoubtedly in his eye when writing "Eloisa and Abelard," which he did at Oxford in 1716, shortly after her going abroad, and which appeared the next year. His passion was not requited, nay, was treated with contempt and ridicule; and he became in after years a bitter enemy and foul-mouthed detractor of the lady, although after her return, in 1718, she resided near him at Twickenham, and they seemed outwardly on good terms.

In 1717, and the succeeding year, Pope lost successively his father, Parnell, Garth, and Rowe, and bitterly felt their loss. He finished, as we have seen, the "Iliad" in 1718; but the fifth and sixth volumes, which were the last, did not appear till 1720. Its success, which at the time was triumphant, roused against him the whole host of envy and detraction. Dennis, and all Grub Street with him, were moved to assail him. Pamphlets after pamphlets were published, all of which, after reading with writhing anguish, Pope had the resolution to bind up into volumes—a great collection of calumny, which he preserved, probably, for purposes of future revenge. His own friends, on the other hand, hailed his work with applause, Gay writing a most graceful and elegant poem, in ottava rima, entitled, "Mr Pope's Welcome

Home from Greece," in which his different friends are pictured as receiving him home on the shores of Britain, after an absence of six years. Bentley, that stern old Grecian, avoided the extremes of a howling Grub Street on the one hand, and a flattering aristocracy on the other, and expressed what is, we think, the just opinion when he said, "It is a pretty poem, but it is not Homer."

In 1721, he issued a selection from the poems of Parnell, and prefixed a very beautiful dedication to the Earl of Oxford, commencing with—

"Such were the notes thy once-loved poet sung,
Till death untimely stopp'd his tuneful tongue.
Oh, just beheld and lost, admired and mourn'd,
With softest manners, gentlest arts adorn'd!"

In 1722, he engaged to translate the "Odyssey." He employed Broome and Fenton as his assistants in the work; and the portions translated by them were thought as good as his. He remunerated them very handsomely. Of this work, the first three quarto volumes appeared in 1725; and the fourth and fifth, which completed the work, the following year. Pope sold the copyright to Lintot for £600.

He was busy at this time, too, with an edition of Shakspeare, not quite worthy of either poet. It appeared in six volumes, quarto, in 1725. His preface was good, but he was deficient in antiquarian lore; and his mortification was extreme when Theobald, destined to figure in "The Dunciad," a mere plodding hack, not only in his "Shakspeare Restored," exposed many blunders in Pope's edition; but issued, some years afterwards, an edition of his own, which was much better received by the public.

In 1726, there was a great gathering of the Tory wits at Twickenham. Swift had come from Ireland, and resided for some time with Pope. Bolingbroke came over occasionally from Dawley; and Gay was often there to laugh with, and be laughed at by, the rest. Swift had "Gulliver's Travels"—the most ingenious and elaborate libel against man and God ever written—in his pocket, nearly ready for publication; and we may conceive the grim, sardonic smile with which he read it to his friends, and their tumultuous mirth. Gay was projecting his "Beggars' Opera," and Pope preparing some of his witty "Miscellanies." At the end of two months, the Dean was hurried home by the tidings of Stella's illness. He left the "Travels" behind him, for the copyright of which Pope procured £300, a sum counted then very large, and which Swift generously handed over to Pope.

In September this year, when returning in Lord Bolingbroke's coach from Dawley, the poet was overturned in a little rivulet near Twickenhan, and nearly drowned. The unfortunate little man! One is reminded of Gulliver's accident in the Brobdignagian cream-pot. In trying to break the glasses of the coach, which were down, he severely cut his right hand, and lost the use of two of his fingers, an addition to his other deformities not very desirable; and we suspect that Pope thought Voltaire (who had met him at Bolingbroke's) but a miserable comforter, when, in a letter of pretended condolence, he asked—"Is it possible that those fingers which have written 'The Rape of the Lock,' and dressed Homer so becomingly in an English coat, should have been so barbarously treated? Let the hand of Dennis or of your poetasters be cut off; yours is sacred." It was perhaps in keeping that those mutilated fingers were soon to be employed in attacking Dennis, and that the embittered poet was about, with the half of his hand, but with the whole of his heart, to write "The Dunciad."

In the end of April 1727, we find Swift again in Twickenham, where his irritation at the continued ascendancy of Sir Robert Walpole served to infuse more venom into the "Miscellanies" concocted between him and Pope, two volumes of which appeared in June this year. Gay, also, and the ingenious and admirable Dr Arbuthnot, contributed their quota to these volumes. Swift speedily fell ill with that giddiness and deafness which were the avant-couriers of his final malady; and in August he left Twickenham, and in October, London and England, for ever.

In these "Miscellanies" there appeared the famous "Memoirs of Martinus Scriblerus," written chiefly by Pope, in which he lashed the various proficients in the bathos, under the names of flying fishes, swallows, parrots, frogs, eels, &c., and appended the initials of well-known authors to each head. This roused Grub Street, whose malice had nearly fallen asleep, into fresh fury, and he was bitterly assailed in every possible form. Like Hyder Ali, he now—to travesty Burke—"in the recesses of a mind capacious of such things, determined to leave all Duncedom an everlasting monument of vengeance, and became at length so confident of his force, so collected in his might, that he made no secret whatever of his dreadful resolution, but, compounding all the materials of fun, sarcasm, irony, and invective, into one black cloud, he hung for a while on the declivities of Richmond Hill; and whilst the authors were idly and stupidly gazing on this menacing meteor which blackened all their horizon, it suddenly burst and poured down the whole of its contents on the garrets of Grub Street. Then issued a scene of (ludicrous) woe, the like of which no eye had seen, no heart conceived, and which no tongue can adequately tell. All the horrors of literary war before known or heard of—(MacFlecknoe, the Rehearsal, &c.)—were mercy to the new tempest of havoc which burst from the brain of this remorseless poet. A storm of universal laughter filled every bookseller's shop, and penetrated into the remotest attics. The miserable dunces, in part, were stricken mad with rage—in part, dumb with consternation. Some fled for refuge to ale, and others to ink; while not a few fell, or feared to fall, into the 'jaws of famine.'" This singular poem was written in 1727. It was first printed surreptitiously (i.e., with the connivance of the author) in Dublin, and then reprinted in London. The first perfect edition, however, did not appear in London till 1729. On the day of its publication, according to Pope, a crowd of authors besieged the publisher's shop; and by entreaties, threats, nay, cries of treason, tried to hinder its appearance. What a scene it must have been—of teeth gnashing above ragged coats, and eyes glaring through old periwigs—of faces livid with famine and ferocity; while, to complete the confusion, hawkers, booksellers, and even lords, were mixed with the crowd, clamouring for its issue! And as, says Pope, "there is no stopping a torrent with a finger, out it came." The consequence he had foreseen. A universal howl of rage and pain burst from the aggrieved dunces, on whose naked sides the hot pitch had fallen. They pushed their rejoinders beyond the limits of civilised literary warfare; and although Pope had been coarse in his language, they were coarser far, and their blackguardism was not redeemed by wit or genius. Pope felt, or seemed to feel, entire indifference as to these assaults. On some of them, indeed, he could afford to look down with contempt, on account of their obvious animus and gross language. Others, again, were neutralised by the fact, that their authors had provoked reprisals by their previous insults or ingratitude to Pope. Many, however, were too obscure for his notice; and some, such as Aaron Hill and Bentley, did not deserve to be classed with the Theobalds and Ralphs. To Hill, he, after some finessing, was compelled to make an apology. Altogether, although this production increased Pope's fame, and the conception of his power, it did not tend to shew him in the most amiable light, or perhaps to promote his own comfort or peace of mind. After having emptied out his bile in "The Dunciad," he ought to have become mellower in temper, and resigned satire for ever. He continued, on the contrary, as ill-natured as before; and although he afterwards flew at higher game, the iron had entered into his soul, and he remained a satirist, and therefore an unhappy man, for life.

In 1731 appeared an "Epistle on Taste," which was very favourably received; only his enemies accused him of having satirised the Duke of Chandos in it, a man who had befriended Pope, and had lent him money. Pope denied the charge, although it is very possible, both from his own temperament, and from the frequent occurrence of similar cases of baseness in literary life, that it may have been true. Nothing is more common than for those who have been most liberally helped, to become first the secret, and then the open, enemies of their benefactors. In 1732 appeared his epistle on "The Use of Riches," addressed to Lord Bathurst. These two epistles were afterwards incorporated in his "Moral Essays."

As far back as 1725, Pope had been revolving the subject of the "Essay on Man;" and, indeed, some of its couplets remind you of "pebbles which had long been rolled over and polished in the ocean of his mind." It has been asserted, but not proved, that Lord Bolingbroke gave him the outline of this essay in prose. It is unquestionable, indeed, that Bolingbroke exercised influence over Pope's mind, and may have suggested some of the thoughts in the Essay; but it is not probable that a man like Pope would have set himself on such a subject simply to translate from another's mind. He published the first epistle of the Essay, in 1732, anonymously, as an experiment, and had the satisfaction to see it successful. It was received with rapture, and passed through several editions ere the author was known; although we must say that the value of this reception is considerably lessened, when we remember that the critics could not have been very acute who did not detect Pope's "fine Roman hand" in every sentence of this brilliant but most unsatisfactory and shallow performance.

In the same year died dear, simple-minded Gay, who found in Pope a sincere mourner, and an elegant elegiast; and on the 7th of June 1733, expired good old Mrs Pope, at the age of ninety-four. Pope, who had always been a dutiful son, erected an obelisk in his own grounds to her memory, with a simple but striking inscription in Latin. During this year, he published the third part of the "Essay on Man," an epistle to Lord Cobham, On the Knowledge and Characters of Man, and an Imitation of the First Satire of the Second Book of Horace. In this last, he attacks, in the most brutal style, his former love Lady Mary W. Montague, who replied in a piece of coarse cleverness, entitled, "Verses to the Imitator of the First Satire of the Second Book of Horace,"—verses in which she was assisted by Lord Harvey, another of Pope's victims. He wrote, but was prudent enough to suppress, an ironical reply.

In 1734 appeared his very clever and highly-finished epistle to Dr Arbuthnot (now entitled the "Prologue to the Satires"), who was then languishing toward death. Arbuthnot, from his deathbed, solemnly advised Pope to regulate his satire, and seems to have been afraid of his personal safety from his numerous foes. Pope replied in a manly but self-defensive style. He is said about this time to have in his walks carried arms, and had a large dog as his protector; but none of the dunces had courage enough to assail him. Dennis, who was no dunce, might have ventured on it—but he had become miserably infirm, poor, and blind; and Pope had heaped coals of fire on his head, by contributing a Prologue to a play which was acted for his behoof.

Our author's life becomes now little else than a record of multiplying labours and increasing infirmities. In 1734 appeared the fourth part of the "Essay on Man," and the Second Satire of the Second Book of Horace. In 1735 were issued his "Characters of Women: An Epistle to a Lady" (Martha Blount). In this appears his famous character of Atossa—the Duchess of Marlborough. It is said—we fear too truly—that these lines being shewn to her Grace, as a character of the Duchess of Buckingham, she recognised in them her own likeness, and bribed Pope with a thousand pounds to suppress it. He did so religiously—as long as she was alive—and then published it! In the same year he printed a second volume of his "Miscellaneous Works," in folio and quarto, uniform with the "Iliad" and "Odyssey," including a versification of the Satires of Donne; also, anonymously, a production disgraceful to his memory, entitled, "Sober Advice from Horace to the Young Gentlemen about Town," in which he commits many gross indecorums of language, and annexes the name of the great Bentley to several indecent notes. It is said that Bentley, when he read the pamphlet, cried, "'Tis an impudent dog, but I talked against his Homer, and the portentous cub never forgives."

The "Essay on Man" and the "Moral Epistles" were designed to be parts of a great system of ethics, which Pope had long revolved in his mind, and wished to incarnate in poetry. At this time occurred the strange, mysterious circumstances connected with the publication of his letters. It seems that, in 1729, Pope had recalled from his correspondents the letters he had written them, of many of which he had kept no copies. He was induced to this by the fact, that after Henry Cromwell's death, his mistress, Mrs Thomas, who was in indigent circumstances, had sold the letters which had passed between Pope and her keeper, to Curll the bookseller, who had published them without scruple. When Pope obtained his correspondence, he, according to his own statement, burned a great many and laid past the others, after having had a copy of them taken, and deposited in Lord Oxford's library. And his charge against Curll was, that he obtained surreptitiously some of these letters, and published them without Pope's consent. But, ere we come to the circumstances of the publication, several other things require to be noticed. In 1733, Curll, anxious to publish a Life of Pope, advertised for information; and, in consequence, one P.T., who professed to be an old friend of Pope's and his father's, wrote Curll a letter, giving an account of Pope's ancestry, which tallied exactly with what Pope himself, in a note to one of his poems, furnished the following year. P.T., in a second letter, offered to the publisher a large collection of Pope's letters, and inclosed a copy of an advertisement he had drawn out to be published by Curll. Strange as it seems, Curll took no notice of the proposal till 1735, when, having accidentally turned up a copy of P.T.'s advertisement, he sent it to Pope, with a letter requesting an interview, and mentioning that he had some papers of P.T.'s in reference to his family history, which he would shew him. Pope replied by three advertisements in the papers, denying all knowledge of P.T. or his collection of letters or MSS. P.T. then wrote Curll that he had printed the letters at his own expense, seeking a sum of money for them, and appointing an interview at a tavern to shew him the sheets. This was countermanded the next day, P.T. professing to be afraid of Pope and his "bravoes," although how Pope was to know of this meeting was, according to Curll, "the cream of the jest."

Soon after, a round, fat man, with a clergyman's gown and a barrister's band, called on Curll, at ten o'clock at night. He said his name was Smith, that he was a cousin of P.T.'s, and shewed the book in sheets, along with about a dozen of the original letters. After a good deal of negotiation with this personage, Curll obtained fifty copies of P.T.'s printed copies, and issued a flaming advertisement announcing the publication of Pope's letters for thirty years, and stating that the original MSS. were lying at his shop, and might be seen by any who chose, although not a single MS. seems to have been delivered. Smith, the day that the advertisement appeared, handed over, for a sum of money, about three hundred volumes to Curll. But as in the advertisement it was stated that various letters of lords were included, and as there is a law amongst regulations of the Upper House that no peer's letters can be published without his consent, at the instance of the Earl of Jersey, and in consequence, too, of an advertisement of Pope's, the books were seized, and Curll, and the printer of the paper where the advertisement appeared, were ordered to appear at the bar for breach of privilege. P.T. wrote Curll to tell him to conceal all that passed between him and the publisher, and promising him more valuable letters still. Curll, however, told the whole story; and as, when the books were examined, not a single lord's letter was found among them, Curll was acquitted, his books restored to him, the lords saying that they had been made the tools of Pope; and he proceeded to advertise the correspondence, in terms most insulting to Pope, who now felt himself compelled (!) to print, by subscription, his genuine letters, which, when printed, turned out, strange to tell, to be identical with those published by the rapacious bookseller! On viewing the whole transaction, we incline with Johnson, Warton, Bowles, Macaulay, and Carruthers, to look upon it as one of Pope's ape-like stratagems—to believe that P.T. was himself, Smith his agent, and that his objects were partly to outwit Curll, to mystify the public, to gratify that strange love of manoeuvring which dwelt as strongly in him as in any match-making mamma, and to attract interest and attention to the genuine correspondence when it should appear. Pope, it was said, could not "drink tea without a stratagem," and far less publish his correspondence without a series of contemptible tricks—tricks, however, in which he was true to his nature—that being a curious compound of the woman and the wit, the monkey and the genius.

In 1737, four of his Imitations of Horace were published, and in the next year appeared two Dialogues, each entitled "1738," which now form the Epilogue to the Satires. One of them was issued on the same day with Johnson's "London." In that year, too, he published his "Universal Prayer,"—a singular specimen of latitudinarian thought, expressed in a loose simplicity of language, quite unusual with its author. The next year he had intended to signalise by a third Dialogue, which he commenced in a vigorous style, but which he did not finish, owing to the dread of a prosecution before the Lords; and with the exception of letters (one of them interesting, as his last to Swift), his pen was altogether idle. In 1740, he did nothing but edit an edition of select Italian Poets. This year, Crousaz, a Swiss professor of note, having attacked (we think most justly) the "Essay on Man" as a mere Pagan prolusion—a thin philosophical smile cast on the Gordian knot of the mystery of the universe, instead of a sword cutting, or trying to cut, it in sunder—Warburton, a man of much talent and learning, but of more astuteness and anxiety to exalt himself, came forward to the rescue, and, with a mixture of casuistical cunning and real ingenuity, tried, as some one has it, "to make Pope a Christian," although, even in Warburton's hands, like the dying Donald Bane in "Waverley," he "makes but a queer Christian after all;" and his system, essentially Pantheistic, contrives to ignore the grand Scripture principles of a Fall, of a Divine Redeemer, of a Future World, and the glorious light or darkness which these and other Christian doctrines cast upon the Mystery of Man. If, however, Warburton, with all his scholastic subtlety, failed to make Pope a Christian, he made him a warm friend; Allen, Pope's acquaintance, a rich father-in-law; and himself, by and by, the Bishop of Gloucester. Sophistry has seldom, although sometimes, been thus richly rewarded.

The last scene of Pope's tiny and tortured existence was now at hand. But ere it closed, it must close like Dryden's, characteristically, with an author's quarrel. Colley Cibber had long been a favourite of Pope's ire, and had as often retorted scorn, till at last, by laughing upon the stage at Pope's play (partly Gay's), entitled, "Three Hours After Marriage," he roused the bard almost to frenzy; and Pope set to work to remodel "The Dunciad;" and, dethroning Theobald, set up Cibber as the lawful King of the Dull, a most unfortunate substitution, since, while Theobald was the ideal of stolid, solemn stupidity, Cibber was gay, light, pert, and clever; full of pluck, too, and who overflowed in reply, with pamphlets which gave Pope both a headache and a heartache whenever he perused them.

Pope had never been strong, and for many years the variety and multitude of his frailties had been increasing. He had habitually all his life been tormented with headaches, for which he found the steam of strong coffee the chief remedy. He had hurt his stomach, too, by indulging in excess of stimulating viands, such as potted lampreys, and in copious and frequent drams. He was assailed at last by dropsy and asthma; and on the 30th of May 1744, he breathed his last, fifty-six years of age. He had long, he said, "been tired of the world," and died with philosophic composure and serenity. He took the sacrament according to the form of the Roman Catholic Church; but merely, he said, because it "looked right." A little before his death, he called for his desk, and began an essay on the immortality of the soul, and on those material things which tend to weaken or to strengthen it for immortality, enumerating generous wines as among the latter influences, and spirituous liquors among the former! His last words were, "There is nothing that is meritorious but virtue and friendship; and, indeed, friendship itself is only a part of virtue." Thus, "motionless and moanless," without a word about Christ—the slightest syllable of repentance—and with a scrap of heathen morality in his mouth, died the brilliant Alexander Pope. Who is ready to say, "May my last end be like his"? His favourite Martha Blount behaved, according to some accounts, with disgusting unconcern on the occasion. So true it is, "there is no friendship among the wicked," even although the heartless Bolingbroke, too, was by, and seems to have succeeded in squeezing out some crocodile tears, as he bent over the dying poet, and said, "O God! what is man?" His remains were, according to his wish, deposited in Twickenham church, near his parents, where the single letter P on the stone alone distinguishes the spot.

Pope's character, apart from his poetry, which we intend criticising in our next volume, was not specially interesting or elevated. He was a spoiled child, a small self-tormentor, full to bursting with petty spites, mean animosities, and unfounded jealousies. While he sought, with the fury of a pampered slave, to trample on those authors that were beneath him in rank or in popularity, he could on all occasions fawn with the sycophancy of a eunuch upon the noble, the rich, and the powerful. Hazlitt speaks of Moore as a "pug-dog barking from the lap of a lady of quality at inferior passengers." The description is far more applicable to Pope. We have much allowance to make for the influence exerted on his mind by his singularly crooked frame and sickly habit of body, by his position as belonging to a proscribed faith, and by his want of training in a public school; but after all these deductions, we cannot but deplore the spectacle of one of the finest, clearest, and sharpest minds that England ever produced, so frequently reminding you of a bright sting set in the body, and steeped in the venom, of a wasp. And yet, withal, he possessed many virtues, which endeared him to a multitude of friends. He was a kind son. He was a faithful and devoted friend. He loved, if not man, yet many men with deep tenderness. A keen politician he was not; but, so far as he went along with his party, he was true to the common cause. In morals, he was greatly superior, in point of external decorum, to most of the wits of the time; but in falsehood, finesse, treachery, and envy, he stood at the bottom of the list, without that plea of poverty, or wretchedness, or despair, which so many of them might have urged. Uneasy, indeed, he always, and unhappy he often, was; but very much of his uneasiness and unhappiness sprung from his own fault. He attacked others, and could not bear to be attacked in return. He was a bully and a coward. He threw himself into a thorn-hedge, and was amazed that he came out covered with scratches and blood. While he shone in satirising many kinds of vice, he laid himself open to retort by his own want of delicacy. He, as well as Swift, was fond of alluding in his verse to polluted and forbidden things. There, and there alone, his taste deserted him; and there is something disgusting and unnatural in the combination of the elegant and the obscene—the coarse in sentiment and the polished in style. And whatever may be said for many of the amiable traits of the Man, there is very little to be said for the general tendency—so far as healthy morality and Christian principle are concerned—of the writings of the Poet.

Alexander Pope – A Concise Bibliography

The Major works
Pastorals (1709)
An Essay on Criticism (1711)
Messiah (1712)
The Rape of the Lock (1712 and enlarged in 1714)
Windsor Forest (1713)
Translation of the Iliad (1715-1720)
Eloisa to Abelard (1717)

Three Hours After Marriage, with others (1717)
Elegy to the Memory of an Unfortunate Lady (1717)
The Works of Shakespear, in Six Volumes (1723-1725)
Translation of the Odyssey (1725-1726)
Peri Bathous, Or the Art of Sinking in Poetry (1727)
The Dunciad (1728)
Essay on Man (1733-1734)
The Prologue to the Satires (1735)

www.ingramcontent.com/pod-product-compliance
Lightning Source LLC
Chambersburg PA
CBHW060100050426
42448CB00011B/2551